ISSACHAR ANOINTING

By

Phillip Rich

Ekklisia Prophetic Apostolic Ministries, Inc.

Published By Ekklisia Ministries, Inc
COPYRIGHT 2004 A. D.

All rights reserved under International Copyright law. No part of this publication may be reproduced, stored in a retrieval system, or transmitted, in whole or in part, in any form or by any means, electronic, mechanical, photocopying, recording or otherwise, without the prior express consent of the publisher. All scripture is the Kings James Version unless otherwise stated. All rights reserved.

Take note that the name satan is not capitalized. We choose not to acknowledge him, even to the point of violating grammatical rules.

THE ISSACHAR ANOINTING

1 Chronicles 12:32; *"And of the children of Issachar, which were men that had understanding of the times, to know what Israel ought to do* [They had discernment, insight, sensitivities, abilities to know what Israel ought to do.]; *the heads of them were two hundred; and all their brethren were at their commandment."*

Issachar was one of the twelve tribes of Israel. They had understanding of the times and seasons. They were very sensitive to know things in the spirit. Some people say that they studied science and knew a lot of natural things but I don't agree with that interpretation. I believe they were a very spiritual people, sensitive to God's direction. They had some insight into things because of their sensitivity to God.

The word *"Issachar"* means reward, compensation, benefit, salary. They were people whose lifestyle rewarded others. Your sensitivity to God is compensation to other Christians because you are able to know things in the Spirit, able to pick up things in the Spirit. You are a blessing and a benefit to other Christians. They may not know it yet but you are.

Prophets and prophetic people are blessings to the Body of Christ because they pick up things in the spirit. They know things. They know what is going on.

Times and seasons are extremely important. If you know to do the right thing at the right time you never miss out on the benefit of the blessing that God has for you. People who don't know the times and seasons miss what God is trying to do, what God is trying to release into their lives. Therefore they don't get the benefits, the compensation, or the rewards.

God rewards our ability to connect with Him at the right time, in the right way. In the natural if you can hit something right on, at the right time, in the right place you can get blessed.

Use the stock market as an example. Make an investment at the right time and see what happens. You also know what happens if you sell that stock at the right time. Times and seasons are everything in business. They are everything in the spirit. There are times when we should be singing a song and times when we should be preaching a message. We have to be sensitive enough with the Issachar anointing to know when to do what, to be singing when we are supposed to be singing, preaching when we are supposed to be preaching and not miss out on those special changes that happen in the spirit.

Ecclesiastes 3 tells us that there is a time and a purpose for everything under heaven. We have to hit those times and seasons right on. To hit a time in the spirit can make the difference between success and failure. God is teaching us that we need to be sensitive to times and seasons in the spirit, to know when something changes and change with it. Flow with it. This is how you get blessed in the natural and in the spirit.

There is a time to pray for somebody, a time to minister to somebody, a time to say a word of knowledge, a time to give a prophecy and a time not to. You can miss those seasons, those timings. If you are right on, people are ready to hear what you have to say and they get the blessing of the Lord.

We know that the heavens open at certain seasons and certain times. Remember the crippled man in the Gospel who was waiting for the stirring of the water to get into the pool? At a certain season an angel would come and trouble the waters. Whoever was the first one into the water after it was troubled was made whole. The man was waiting for it but his timing was always off. He never hit it right on. The Lord is showing us that we need the Issachar anointing. We need to know when something is happening in the Spirit, when we should or should not be doing something. Those things are extremely important and God wants us to be sensitive to those things.

Burden Bearer

When we look at the father's blessing that was released when Israel (Jacob) blessed all of his twelve sons, we see that when he blessed Issachar he described some things about him.

Genesis 49:14-15; *"Issachar is a strong ass couching down between two burdens: And he saw that rest was good, and the land that it was pleasant; and bowed his shoulder to bear, and became a servant unto tribute."*

This means Issachar was a worker, a beast of burden, a laborer who was able to get under heavy loads and help to carry them. Jacob was saying that Issachar was strong and able to carry a heavy load.

There are many Christians to whom you cannot go and tell your needs because they are too weak to handle it. The only thing they can ever hear you say is something positive. You cannot go to them, lay a heavy load on them, and ask them to pray with you and help you carry that thing in the spirit. Some people can't handle it. The sons of Issachar can because they are people of prayer, a people who are sensitive to God. They don't mind getting under a load. They don't mind hearing your problem and praying with you. They will stay with you in prayer and continue to pray with you until you come out of that thing.

Part of the Issachar anointing is an intercessory anointing, an ability to carry the burdens of others. The Bible says that we are supposed to bear one another's burdens and so fulfill the law of Christ. It is more than knowing the times and seasons. It is also having a strength in you that makes you able to bear one another's burdens and so fulfill the law of Christ. You are able to get under someone else's burdens with them, be strong, and help them carry that thing. God wants us to understand the Issachar anointing fully.

Issachar sees the good, that which is pleasant in the land. He gets his shoulder under a load to make things better. An Issachar anointing is found in someone who is able and willing to get under a load and make things better.

I have been in churches where people didn't want to help you start a church or to be a part of a small church. They wanted to go where someone else was carrying the load, someone else was paying the tithe, someone else was giving the offering, someone else was cleaning the bathrooms, and someone else was doing all the work. All they had to do was come in, sit in a nice chair and not do anything but benefit from someone else's labor. There are churches filled with people like that and that is not the Issachar anointing.

Remember, Issachar sees the good in a situation and yet wants to make it better. They want to be a part of what is necessary to build something, to do something and to be involved in something. The Issachar anointing is found in someone who is willing to bear the burden, willing to get in there and work to see what good can come out of hard labor.

Can you come into your church, see the big picture of what God is doing, get your arm and shoulder under the load, put your shoulder to the wheel, your hand to the plow and your heart to the plan of God? If you can do that you can help build the vision that your church has. You have to see the good. Part of the Issachar anointing is being able to see in the spirit what God is trying to build before it is even built. You help make it that way.

In Genesis 49, we saw Israel (Jacob) speaking a blessing over Issachar. He said that Issachar was willing to become a servant, even a servant under tribute. He was willing to see the good, get his shoulder under that responsibility. Even if the labor is taxing, even if it costs something he is still willing to be a servant. He is still willing to get in there and make something good out of it.

Many have been called into the Issachar anointing, but you have to recognize what it is. Realize that you are not being taken advantage of but you are being developed. You are becoming somebody who can help a situation become what it is supposed to be. It takes work. It takes someone willing to be a servant even if it is taxing, even if it is hard, even if at times it is difficult. Tribute means to be taxed.

There are a lot of people who don't desire the Issachar anointing. They can't visualize what God is doing. They don't want to start small. They don't want to build something. They don't want to get in and do something. They are not willing to be a servant under tribute. They are not willing to carry a load. Yet all of that is part of the Issachar anointing of discerning times and seasons and seeing things in the spirit. You have to be so sensitive to God that you can see what God is doing before you can see it in the natural. You get a glimpse of what God is building. You get a glimpse of what God is doing.

A Place to Function

Deuteronomy 33:18-19; *"And of Zebulun he said, Rejoice, Zebulun, in thy going out; and, Issachar, in thy tents. They shall call the people unto the mountain; there they shall offer sacrifices of righteousness* [praise and worship]***: for they shall suck of the abundance of the seas, and of treasures hid in the sand."***

Issachar dwelt in tents while others went about doing their own thing. Dwelt in tents means they knew how to stay and function in their place. They knew where to function and where they belonged. God wants you to understand your function, to know where you are to function.

"They shall call the people unto the mountain" means calling the people into prayer and into praise. Issachar calls people higher unto God. Issachar is pointing people to the Lord and drawing them into praise, into worship, into prayer, calling God's people to be closer to God than they have ever been before. The Issachar anointing calls other people into prayer and praise, calls them to join with you. Issachar has a desire to draw others with them closer to the Lord.

"…for they shall suck of the abundance of the seas, and of treasures hid in the sand." Issachar will be able to draw the prosperity out. Issachar has an anointing because they are so dedicated to God that they know how to draw finances out of the spirit. God will show them how to tap in.

Sons of Issachar understand seedtime and harvest. They understand investing into the kingdom. They understand giving. They know how to tap into God's abundance. It doesn't bother them to give a sacrificial seed because they know where it came from in the first place. The sons of Issachar know how to get into the spirit, how to give that seed, believe God and get the wealth that is necessary to do the work of the Lord.

They understand things others don't understand. They understand that sacrificing and giving to God is not losing money. It is investing. It is operating principles that will cause them to pull finances right out of the spirit and to get what is necessary in their lives.

You grow and develop into that anointing. You are not afraid to give an offering, to sacrifice, to plant a seed. There is more where that came from. It doesn't bother you. You are not like other Christians who love money, love things, and don't have any faith in God so they can't give anything to God. The Issachar anointing knows how to get the money. In the spirit they know how to operate the principles and they do operate them. They have insight into the spirit, into the realm of God and into the realm of financial blessing. It is all connected with the Issachar anointing.

You find hidden treasures in the sand that other Christians cannot find. Other Christians do not understand the principles. They can't get it. They miss it. It is too simple for them. They can't just believe God and plant a seed. They can't release what is in their hand because they think that is all they are going to have. They see giving as losing money that they will never see again. That is not what God's Word teaches.

Sensitivity

So, we have to enter into the Issachar anointing and have a sensitivity to discern times and seasons. You see into the spirit and see the way things really are in the spirit realm. You discern seedtimes and harvest in order to be able to plant and reap at the right time. You do it all by faith.

In the spirit, prophetic people are of the tribe of Issachar. We see things, know things, and understand things in the spirit realm.

1 Chronicles 7:5; *"And their brethren among all the families of Issachar were valiant men of might, reckoned in all by their genealogies fourscore and seven thousand."*

They were recorded here as warriors who were brave, strong and mighty in battle. You have a vengeance against demonic spirits.

If you are sensitive to the realm of the spirit, sensitive to the times and seasons, sensitive to know things that others would not know, to pick up things that others do not pick up you have an Issachar anointing in your life. You know where you belong and you know where you fit.

Other Christians are not able to understand prophetic people. They are from another tribe in the spirit, so to speak. You are prophetic so you are Issachar. You have to understand who you are so you will not be moved by other people who expect you to be something else. Prophetic people should know who they are because other people need Issachar to give them direction. The other eleven tribes would come to Issachar for direction because Issachar could see into the spirit. Issachar understood and was sensitive to the times and seasons, sensitive to the things of God, to the ways of the spirit.

Draw upon that Issachar anointing and recognize you have a sensitivity that will allow you to pick up things in the spirit that others won't. ==You will see things, know things in advance, see things happening, see things coming.== You will be sensitive to see how God is moving, when God is moving, and how to move with God when others are pulling their hair out because they do not know what to do. You have the Issachar anointing. You know. You get into the spirit and find out. It will be plain to you and you can point out to them what is happening and what they can do.

As we saw in 1 Chronicles 12, they will come to your commandment. In other words, they will come to you to get a word on what to do with their life, what to do with their future, what to do with certain things and certain situations. *"How do I face this? How do I face that? What do I do when a strange spirit attacks me during the night? I am facing a financial battle, how do I make it through that?"* The Issachar anointing enables you to give direction to other Christians who do not have a clue as to what to do.

You are sensitive to times and seasons. You are sensitive to the principles of God. You are sensitive to deliverance ministry. You are sensitive to warfare. You are sensitive to see the way to get the finances when others don't have a clue. God has made you sensitive. You are Issachar.

There were twelve tribes in Israel in the natural. In the spirit there also are different Christians who function in different ways.

Issachar is not moved by circumstances because Issachar is marching to the beat of a different drummer. Issachar already knows what is happening in the spirit and will operate accordingly. Others get worried and wonder what they are going to do. That is no problem for you and me because we are going to do this and this and this.

You just tell them we are going to pray, get close to God, plant seeds of faith, press into the Lord Jesus Christ, go into the world and preach the gospel to every creature. That is what we are going to do. We are going to take this world for Jesus Christ. While the other Christians are pulling their hair out wondering what they are going to do, you already know what you are going to do. You have already been in the spirit. You know times and seasons and you know what needs to be done. You are Issachar. You are a leader. You are tapped into the things of the spirit. Times and seasons are not baffling to you.

You are not worried about the economy because you have insight that others don't have. You are not worried about what is happening with wars and rumors of wars. You know that the Bible says those things will happen. It doesn't move you. They talk about all the horrible things that are going to happen. "*No, no, no. God is going to take care of me. He is setting some things up here. If you will listen to what I have to tell you, you will be okay too.*" You speak peace to people. Other Christians are thinking holocaust, nightmares, and all those things. You just calm them down and say, "*Wait a minute, we are in the cleft of the rock. Just settle down. Chill out on this thing.*" Issachar does not freak out. They are calm, cool. They are in their own tents. That means they are not running around pulling their hair out. They know what is going on. They have chilled out in God. They have understanding. They have the wisdom of the Lord. They have direction from God. They are walking in the ways of the Lord and are not worrying.

I am not worrying about the economy because I am not operating according to it anyway. I am Issachar. I know how to pull the finances out of the spirit realm. I can find the hidden treasures in the sand that other people don't even know about. I can get finances when nobody else can.

I am Issachar. I know times and seasons, I know how things operate in the spirit. I am a warrior. I am brave. Big deal if the devil shows up. We are going to kick his butt, get him out of the way and go on down the road. We are not worried about what the devil is doing. We deal with him because we have authority over him.

We are Issachar. We are brave. We are strong. We are mighty. We are not fearful. We are not doubters or pouters or do-with-outers. People ask what we are going to do about the economy. I don't know what you are going to do but I do know what I am going to do. I am going to believe God. I am going to operate God's principles and my

God is going to supply all that I need. I don't know what you are going to do if you don't serve the God that I serve and if you don't do the principles that I do to get what I am going to get and to have what I have. But if you want to find out how, follow me and I will show you.

We are supposed to be examples to lead people into the blessing of God, to give them commandment. They will listen to the sons of Issachar because the sons of Issachar know what they are doing. We are not caught unaware. We are very much aware and we are confident. The world may call us a little cocky. That's all right. We just know who we are. We have insight. We have seen ahead. We see into the spirit the way things really are. Other Christians don't. They see Satan's smokescreen. They see fear. They see doubt. They see unbelief. But they don't see things the way they really are. Issachar sees God's Word and says this is the way it is. It is exactly the way God says it and it is no other way. We are confident in our God. We are strong and we do exploits in God.

Use your spiritual senses and sense faith, direction, the hand of God moving. Sense God's will that is taking place, sense the good that is going to happen. Sense those things. See God at work behind the scenes. In the midst of everything God is always moving. God is not confused, not bound up, not hindered. God has no shortages or lack. Why should we be acting any different than the sons of Issachar act? We know who we are. We know what we are doing. We are in faith. Our God is seeing us through. We know what to do if things get tight. We know how to operate the principles. We know how to pull some finances out of the spirit. We know how to get it. We have all operated the principles and seen financial blessing come our way. That is the sons of Issachar blessing.

We know our God. We operate the principles. If we have a need we know what to do about it. We are not moved. The same way it has worked before, it will work again. Keep operating those principles. Keep on believing God. Be confident of your sensitivity in God. God gave it to you. It will bring you through. It will bring you out and it will set other people free. This is a word of encouragement to the church.

You have the inside information, the insight when others don't have a clue. It works and there is confidence. You are bold and you are mighty. You are a warrior.

You help others go up to the mountain of God and worship the Lord. You encourage others.

Issachar sees into the spirit and knows that it is more real that the natural. Don't put your confidence in the flesh. Don't put your confidence in what you see with your natural eyes, what you hear with your natural ears. Those things are temporary. Put your confidence in what you see in the spirit.

As you operate more and more in the Issachar anointing, more people will come to you because you know things. They will come to you to get words of wisdom. They will come to you to have prayer. They will come to you to be strengthened.

The sons of Issachar have the anointing to be able to look into the spirit and to have insight into what is happening. Now let's look at the five areas we can have insight into.

The Signs of the Times

Luke 12:54-56; *"And he said also to the people, When ye see a cloud rise out of the west, straightway ye say, There cometh a shower; and so it is. And when ye see the south wind blow, ye say, There will be heat; and it cometh to pass. Ye hypocrites, ye can discern the face of the sky and of the earth; but how is it that ye do not discern this time?"*

Jesus was saying that there are people who can look and read the weather by looking at the outward signs but they cannot get into the spirit and read the signs of the times. God wants us to be very sensitive to what is happening in the spirit realm and not be caught unaware of what is taking place in the world. I believe we should know before anyone else knows. The church should never be ignorant of what is going to come upon the earth. We should be able to be so sensitive to the spirit that we are able to read things in the spirit and know what is going to happen.

When I played football as a middle linebacker, I had to be able to read the play ahead of time and tell everybody else what was going to be happening. My ability to read that play would determine if I was going to tackle the guy with the football and not allow him to get a touchdown. I had to defensively be able to read that play ahead of time and alert the players as to what was happening. I had to see a couple of quick little moves and what they were doing and be able to tell the guys what was going on.

God wants us to be like that in the spirit. He wants us to read things in the spirit, not be weird with it but really see and understand what God is doing and what is happening in the earth. Then to be able to alert the Body of Christ as to what is happening. The children of Issachar were able to do that and the people listened to them because they were so proficient in it.

Times and Seasons

We are supposed to be able to discern the times and the seasons, be able to catch those things and read them in the spirit. It is an anointing that God has given to his people. We have to be aware that it is available. Usually we get tripped up because we are lulled to sleep in the spirit. We are not aware of things. We are not taking time to pray and to seek the Lord about what is happening in the spirit, seek Him about the future. It takes time to be able to read those things in the spirit. You have to take time to talk to God and ask Him to reveal it to you.

You have not because you ask not. A lot of times people don't flow in the spirit because they don't ask God to give anything to them. If you don't ask for a word of knowledge, you probably will never have one. It is that simple. Just little simple truths.

If you ever ask God to reveal something to you, He will. He wants to. But what most of us do is think, well, God is God and if He wants to reveal something to me He will. If He doesn't want to, He won't. In reality, that is not scripture. He said He would lead us into all truth and show us things that we don't know. But there is one little point that I found out. We must ask Him for it and we must seek Him for it. If you don't ask, He is not going to tell you. If you don't seek, the Word of God says you won't find. You have to ask, you have to seek and then He begins to unveil those things to you.

People

The next thing we are going to look at is that we must be able to discern the people who should or should not be in our lives.

When God wants to bless you He will send someone across your pathway. When the devil wants to mess you up, he will also send someone across your pathway. You have to be aware of who is coming into your life, who is being sent, and who is sending them. You must discern who is who and be able to work with or avoid certain people in your life. People will either draw you closer to God or take you further away from God at all times.

Jesus was very proficient at discerning people in His life.

John 2:23-25; *"Now when he was in Jerusalem at the passover, in the feast day, many believed in his name, when they saw the miracles which he did. But Jesus did not commit himself unto them, because he knew all men, And needed not that any should testify of man: for <u>he knew what was in man</u>."*

Jesus did not commit Himself to those people because He knew what was in them. He knew their purpose. He knew who was sending whom. You and I need to become so keen in the spirit that we can spot those who are sent to us by God and spot those who are plantings of Satan sent into our life.

One good way to find out is to check your own heart after an encounter or two with them. After some form of involvement with these people, do you find yourself getting closer to God? Or do you find yourself slipping away a little bit from the Lord? Do you find yourself reading the

Bible more because of that individual who has come into your life? Do you find yourself being more faithful to the House of God? Do you find yourself more obedient to the Word of God? Or do you find the opposite? These are things that we must be very, very keen on. It can make the difference between you going on and becoming what God wants you to be or you being hindered and maybe even side-tracked.

Remember God brings people into our lives but there are also seasons when He takes people out of our lives. We have to be smart enough to discern what is happening. We have to be sharp enough to know what is going on in the realm of the spirit. It is very important. People can either make you or break you if you are not careful. Proverbs 13:20 tells us that if we run with the wise we become wise. If we run with fools we will be destroyed. That is a blanket statement for all children of God.

There are only two kinds of people you should ever associate with. People you can help spiritually or people who can help you spiritually. Nobody else should be in your life. Are you hearing this wisdom? If you can't help them spiritually, then they will drag you down. If they can't help you spiritually, then what are they doing in your life? They are taking away.

God is giving us wisdom concerning discerning people. Only make connections, only associate intimately, and only buddy up with people who you can help spiritually or they can help you spiritually. If they are neither of those then already they are not to be in your life.

Run with the wise and you will be wise. Run with fools and you will be destroyed. Why, because the Bible says fools are destroyed. You become like the company you keep. If you can't help somebody spiritually, they are not going to be helping you. I am talking about somebody who is lost or a weak Christian. Please understand that through we are supposed to be friends with the world, we are not supposed to be buddies with the world. A buddy is someone you hang out with. God never told us to hang out with the world. He told us to be a witness to the world. We can be a friend but not a buddy. A buddy hangs out and does whatever the buddies are doing. Those things will take away from your life. Those things will hinder your walk in God.

Though we want to witness to the world and affect the world, we are in the world but not of the world. We don't want the world to be converting us while we are trying to witness to them. We don't want to lose our witness while we are trying to be a witness. We don't want to lose our walk with God and our precious relationship with the Lord while we are trying to win the world. If we understand the balance, it will never happen. We won't be drawn down if we know the balance and can discern people.

Jesus did not commit Himself to everybody because He knew what was in them. The Lord wants us to be so keen in the spirit that we don't just commit ourselves to everybody we know. We are keen, we are sharp, we pray and we listen to the inner witness. The Spirit of the Lord within your spirit will bear witness. You will know inside. There is a still small voice inside that will tell you not to hang around with those people. It will be a big yuck within you. You can override it and your life becomes yuck.

We can witness to the world without becoming like the world. We don't want to lose all the great things God has done in us. We want our life to shine before men so they can see our good works and glorify the Father who is in heaven. We don't want to be influenced so much by the world that we begin to act like them and lose our testimony. We are supposed to be a light to them, be a witness to them, share Jesus with them and let them see our light.

But there is a line that must be drawn that we don't step beyond. We must stay in the safety zone of God's presence, His will and His love. To step over the line means that I tarnish my walk with God and I am not going to do that. It is too precious to lose. I must guard it. Whatever you don't guard, you lose in the spirit. You have to protect what is precious. Protect it. Keep it.

Jesus didn't commit Himself to all men because He knew what was in them. God wants us to know what is in them. He wants us to discern a wrong spirit or discern a right one.

One way you can tell when a wrong spirit is that the world is going to want you to do what they are doing. If you don't do what they are doing then all of a sudden they want to write you off. If that is their attitude, then they are the wrong people in your life.

If I have to do what the world is doing in order for them to like me, then they are just going to have to not like me. I am not going to sin with them to try to win them. I am not going to do drugs with them in order to tell them about Jesus. I am not going to do the sin that they do in order to be an influence because already I have lost my influence. Now they're influencing me.

We must discern the heart of man and we can through the Issachar anointing. Through this prophetic anointing we can discern what is in the heart of man. Jesus did and He wants us to do it. It is important for our ability to thrive in the spirit and touch the lives of people.

Things

We must be able to discern things.

1 Corinthians 2:7-16; *"But we speak the wisdom of God in a mystery, even the hidden wisdom, which God ordained before* *the world unto our glory: Which none of the princes of this world knew: for had they known it, they would not have crucified the Lord of glory. But as it is written, Eye hath not seen, nor ear heard, neither have entered into the heart of man, the <u>things</u> which God hath prepared for them that love him. But God hath revealed them unto us by his Spirit: for the Spirit searcheth all <u>things</u>, yea, the deep things of God. For what man knoweth the <u>things</u> of a man, save the spirit of man which is in him? even so the <u>things</u> of God knoweth no man, but the Spirit of God. Now we have received, not the spirit of the world, but the spirit which is of God; that we might know the things that are freely given to us of God. Which things also we speak, not in the words which man's wisdom teacheth, but which the Holy Ghost teacheth; comparing spiritual things with spiritual. But the natural man receiveth not the things of the Spirit of God: for they are foolishness unto him: neither can he know them, because they are spiritually* *discerned. But he that is spiritual judgeth all things, yet he himself is judged of no man. For who hath known the mind of the Lord, that he may instruct him? But we have the mind of Christ."*

We are not talking about people but about things. It is time to discern which things are of God and are not of God. They could even be things that people put into their houses. We can discern if a thing is or is not of God. Some things have satanic symbols on them and demonic spirits are attracted to them.

I believe that we are supposed to be sensitive enough to the Spirit of God and by the Spirit of God to be able to know those things that are of God and those things that are not of God. If something has been dedicated to the devil and there are demonic spirits connected to it, we should be able to pick that up and say, *"By the Spirit of the Lord, this thing is not of God, so I am getting rid of it."* Or *"By the Spirit of the*

Lord, this thing is dedicated to the Lord. It is a good thing. I sense angelic presence around it. I sense it attracts the presence of God."

We have to be sensitive to all different kinds of things. Music is a thing and we need to be sensitive to what types of music are of God and what types of music are not.

We have to be sensitive on all different levels when it comes to things, be able to pick up and discern them. This is done by the Spirit of God.

The Spirit of God will give you understanding. Some things are cut and dried. A lot of times there may be something that looks legitimate and looks good in the natural but in the spirit we come back to the yuck. We can pick up that there is something not good about it. I learned a long time ago, when in doubt throw it out. It is better just to get rid of it, whatever thing it might be. We must be able to connect or disconnect and to be able to know what is happening in the spirit in order to be able to discern things.

Places

Now let's look at places.

Genesis 28:10-22; *"And Jacob went out from Beersheba, and went toward Haran. And he lighted upon a certain place, and tarried there all night, because the sun was set; and he took of the stones of that place, and put them for his pillows, and lay down in that place to sleep* [notice he is in a place here]. *And he dreamed, and behold a ladder set up on the earth, and the top of it reached to heaven: and behold the angels of God ascending and descending on it. And, behold, the LORD stood above it, and said, I am the LORD God of Abraham thy father, and the God of Isaac: the land whereon thou liest, to thee will I give it, and to thy seed; And thy seed shall be as* *the dust of the earth, and thou shalt spread abroad to the west, and to the east, and to the north, and to the south: and in thee and in thy seed shall all the families of the earth be blessed. And, behold, I am with thee, and will keep thee in all places whither thou goest, and will bring thee again into this land; for I will not leave thee, until I have done that which I have spoken to thee of. And Jacob awaked out of his sleep, and he said, Surely the LORD is in this place; and I knew it not* [he did not discern it]. *And he was afraid, and said, How dreadful is this place! this is none other but the house of God, and this is the gate of heaven. And Jacob rose up early in the morning, and <u>took the stone that he had put for his pillows, and set it up for a pillar</u>, and poured oil upon the top of it. And he called the name of that place Bethel: but the name of that city was called Luz at the first. And Jacob vowed a vow, saying, If God will be with me, and will keep me in this way that I go, and will give me bread to eat, and raiment to put on, So* *that I come again to my father's house in peace; then shall the LORD be my God: And this stone, which I have set for a pillar* [it had been a pillow first]*, shall be God's house: and of all that thou shalt give me I will surely give the tenth unto thee."*

There is a discernment that is needed to discern places in the spirit, places where God wants you to connect. When God wants you in a place, it is part of your blessing and it becomes an opening into the heavens for you. It may not be an open heaven for everybody. You have to discern your place. That place is a place of a pillow that becomes a pillar. It is a place of rest in the spirit for you. It is also a pillar, a place for you to dwell where there is safety and security.

If God has connected you to a church, you need to discern that. You have to know that it is the place of the pillow and the pillar and not let the devil displace you. Satan wants to displace you out of the holy place.

It is called a holy place if it is the place where God wants you. It will become Bethel for you. You have to become sensitive enough to know that the angels will ascend and descend where God wants you. God will speak to you a promise about your life just like he did with Jacob. There is a promise connected to the place where you are supposed to be a promise for your life, prophecy, is connected to it.

At the place where Jacob was, the heavens opened and a ladder came down with angels ascending and descending. The ascending and descending means the angels are coming your way to bring blessing and to bring help. They are going back to take anything necessary in the way of requests or prayers that you may be sharing or something you may be requiring of the Lord. You have to discern your place because there is an open heaven there for you. Angels are available to help you.

At the top of the ladder the Lord is speaking a word to you. All of that happened in Genesis 28. Jacob named that place Bethel. He said, *"Here I heard the Lord. Here I visit the Lord. Here I encounter God."*

We have to be sensitive enough to know places because there are places that are dedicated to God and God's presence dwells there. There is a heightened open heaven anointing there.

I also believe that if you are living in a house God has put you in, there should be an open heaven above that house. If there is not, you can make it that way. You can cleanse it so it can be a place of an open heaven. Once you do a little house cleaning and take care of things, it can be that way. There is supposed to be an open heaven where you are so that you can talk to God. You can pray and there will be angels ascending and descending upon you. You are supposed to establish an open heaven where you live.

Your home where you live but it should also be where you pray, where you wait on God, where you relax, where you press into His presence. We need an abiding anointing of the presence of God and an open heaven over our homes. It can be that way. It is supposed to be that way. If you are dedicated, sanctified to the Lord then the place where you dwell is sanctified, holy because you are holy. You can walk in and establish holiness. You can walk in and establish righteousness because there is righteousness in you.

Don't dwell in someone's house where there is not an open heaven. Don't dwell in someone's house where instead of the gates of heaven, the gates of hell are opened up. You will come under an attack that you shouldn't have to come under.

There is a difference between going and witnessing at someone else's house and hanging out. You don't want to hang out where the gate of hell is open because you will be attacked and have losses in your life that will pull you down. You can go and witness there but not hang out. You only want to hang out where the gates of heaven are open and the angels are ascending and descending. If you can't sense angelic presence in your home or in someone else's home, then there is something wrong and must be changed. If it is your home, you need to cleanse it. Cleanse the airways and rededicate it. If it is someone else's home, just don't go back.

As soon as Jacob found out that it was a holy place and called it the House of the Lord, he made a vow. He told the Lord that wherever there was an open heaven, he would bless that place.

People are also doorways and we have to be able to discern people. We have to discern when God sends men and women of God our way. You have to look beyond the flesh and see the gift. The Bible tells us to know no man after the flesh. It is important because even though we know they are housed in flesh, we have to look beyond the house of flesh and see the gift of God within. Once you see the gift of God within, you bless the gift. Pray for that person, support that person and bless that person.

You do whatever you can to bless it when you see God in it. **Whatever you bless that God has blessed, it blesses you.** Whatever God has put His hand to, you want to put your hand also in blessing. Whatever God has blessed, bless what He has blessed and you will get blessed by the blessing. Bless the place that God blesses and you will get blessed by the blessing. Bless the people God has blessed, the people God has put His hand on, the ones He is using, the ones to whom He is pouring out His Spirit, His revelation, the ones He is pouring His very presence through. Bless them and you get blessed by the blessing that God has blessed them with.

When I go somewhere and I sense the blessing of God upon the people, upon the place, I do all that I can to be a blessing to them. By blessing them, I get blessed. When you bless what God has blessed you get blessed by the blessing that God has blessed that person or place with.

We have to learn to operate in discernment and understanding.

When Jacob saw that it was a blessed place and God was there, he began to immediately make plans to bless it. *"I make a vow, I want to start giving. I want to start blessing it."* Why did he do that? Because, he discerned.

When you sit under a ministry somewhere and the blessing of God is all over them, you are getting blessed in that ministry so turn around and be a blessing. If

God sends somebody across my path and I discern that they are of God, I discern the blessing of God is upon them, I discern the presence of God upon them, I discern the angelic hosts are all around them I will do something to bless them. I will not let them get out of my sight or away from me without me doing something.

The children of Issachar blessing is a blessing to be able to be sensitive in the realm of the spirit and to be able to discern things, people, places, even seasons and times. For everything there is a season, a time for every purpose under heaven. We must be sensitive to those seasons and times. We must be sensitive to purposes, people, things and places. It will make all the difference to you in being blessed or not being blessed. Just the discerning of these things can put you over or hinder you. This message is vital to your success in God, your ability to win, your ability to go forth and do great things in the kingdom of God.